Vocabulary Teaching Handbook

OXFORD PICTURE DICTIONARY

SECOND EDITION

Jayme Adelson-Goldstein

T0369882

OXFORD
UNIVERSITY PRESS

198 Madison Avenue
New York, NY 10016 USA

Great Clarendon Street, Oxford OX2 6DP UK

Oxford University Press is a department of the University of Oxford.
It furthers the University's objective of excellence in research,
scholarship, and education by publishing worldwide in

Oxford   New York
Auckland   Cape Town   Dar es Salaam   Hong Kong   Karachi
Kuala Lumpur   Madrid   Melbourne   Mexico City   Nairobi
New Delhi   Shanghai   Taipei   Toronto

With offices in
Argentina   Austria   Brazil   Chile   Czech Republic   France   Greece
Guatemala   Hungary   Italy   Japan   Poland   Portugal   Singapore
South Korea   Switzerland   Thailand   Turkey   Ukraine   Vietnam

OXFORD and OXFORD ENGLISH are registered trademarks of
Oxford University Press.

© Oxford University Press 2009

Database right Oxford University Press (maker)

All rights reserved. No part of this publication may be reproduced,
stored in a retrieval system, or transmitted, in any form or by any means,
without the prior permission in writing of Oxford University Press (with
the sole exception of photocopying carried out under the conditions
stated in the paragraph headed "Photocopying"), or as expressly
permitted by law, or under terms agreed with the appropriate copyright
clearance organization. Enquiries concerning reproduction outside the
scope of the above should be sent to the ELT Rights Department, Oxford
University Press, at the address above.

You must not circulate this book in any other binding or cover
and you must impose this same condition on any acquirer.

Photocopying

The Publisher grants permission for the photocopying of those pages
marked "photocopiable" according to the following conditions.
Individual purchasers may make copies for their own use or for use by
classes that they teach. School purchasers may make copies for use by
staff and students, but this permission does not extend to additional
schools or branches.

Under no circumstances may any part of this book be photocopied
for resale.

Any websites referred to in this publication are in the public domain and
their addresses are provided by Oxford University Press for information
only. Oxford University Press disclaims any responsibility for the content.

Editorial Director: Laura Pearson
Executive Publishing Manager: Stephanie Karras
Managing Editor: Sharon Sargent
Associate Development Editor: Charlotte Roh
Design Director: Susan Sanguily
Design Manager: Maj-Britt Hagsted
Senior Designer: Michael Steinhofer
Design Assistant: Karen Vanderbilt
Project Coordinator: Sarah Dentry
Cover Design: Stacy Merlin
Image Editor: Robin Fadool
Manufacturing Manager: Shanta Persaud
Manufacturing Coordinator: Faye Wang

ISBN: 978 019 474024 1   OPD Vocabulary Teaching Handbook 2e

Printed in China

10 9 8 7

Photos by: Jayme Adelson-Goldstein: 13; 15; 16; AGE FotoStock: John Birdsall, 32;
The Image Works: Bob Daemmrich, 4; Dennis Kitchen: 26.

Illustrations by: Lori Anazalone: 14 (weather map); Philip Batini/AA Reps: 19;
Composure Graphics: 9; 12; 27; 33; Mike Gardner: 32 (bottom left); Glenn
Gustafson: 19 (top right); Janos Jantner/Beehive Illustration: 11;14; 25; Graham
Kennedy: 18; Mark Reidy/Scott Hull Associates: 20; Zina Saunders: 29; Anna
Veltfort: 28 (top); 29 (bottom); Brad Walker: 24; William Waitzman: 28
(bottom).

Cover art by CUBE/Illustration Ltd. (hummingbird); 9 Surf Studios
(lettering).

Table of Contents

Welcome to the *OPD Vocabulary Teaching Handbook*

We know that language acquisition is a multifaceted process and that there are a variety of ways for learners to acquire the skills, vocabulary, and structures they need to be fluent in English. While it would be wonderful to claim there is "one best way" to learn English, we cannot. We can, however, incorporate different ESL techniques and strategies into our instructional repertoire so that our teaching corresponds to our students' diverse learning styles and goals.

The Oxford Picture Dictionary Second Edition Vocabulary Teaching Handbook includes numerous vocabulary learning strategies, lesson techniques, and activities, as well as an overview of the principles and research on which they're based. This book's goal is to provide professional development to help you help your learners increase their active vocabulary and, by extension, develop stronger listening, speaking, reading, and writing skills in English.

Research shows that the most successful professional development involves an ongoing, critically reflective approach.[1] To that end, this program offers both interpersonal and intrapersonal opportunities to learn about, apply, reflect on and refine your instructional techniques. Feasibly, you could work through this material in your pajamas on a lazy Sunday afternoon of lesson planning, or, just as easily, use the materials as the foundation for a study circle with your colleagues (in perhaps slightly more formal attire).

How does this program work?

Each section of the *Vocabulary Teaching Handbook* covers material critical to helping learners increase their active vocabulary:

- What words do learners need?
- What strategies can learners use?
- How do I create communicative vocabulary lessons?
- How can I integrate vocabulary activities into every lesson?
- What resources are available to help me learn more?

Study circle members often read current research and then meet to discuss their experiences in applying the research to their instruction.

Within each section are tasks to help you adapt and apply the information you've learned to your own classes. You'll also find questions that prompt you to reflect on your own and your learners' responses to different types of vocabulary instruction.

Working alone or with a study circle, you can determine which sections are most meaningful for you and tackle those first. The research references listed on pages 38–39 provide deeper analysis of the theories that underpin the strategies, techniques, and activities explored in this book.

Do I need special materials?

While all the examples and illustrations in the *Vocabulary Teaching Handbook* are from the *Oxford Picture Dictionary* program, the techniques, strategies, lessons, and activities presented here are not dependent on having the *OPD*. To try out the activities in the *Handbook* with your class, you will need sets of pictures or picture cards for the target vocabulary items and thematic illustrations that can prompt speaking and writing, such as a picture of workers in a restaurant or a scene of people engaged in recreational activities at a park. The only other requirements are a means of demonstrating or conducting activities in front of the whole class (e.g., chalkboard, whiteboard, electronic whiteboard, overhead projector, butcher paper). It's not necessary to have a copier; learners can make their own worksheets, and many learners benefit from the kinesthetic activity of copying words and pictures onto their own papers. However, making copies of the activity worksheets will reduce in-class preparation time and leave more time for the activity itself.

How much time will this program take?

Working through the information and sample lessons and activities in this *Handbook* should take no more than an hour or so. One of the great benefits of completing a self-directed professional development program is the flexibility you have to select when and how to complete the application tasks and reflections. Allocating a week for each section of this book should allow sufficient time to:

- Read and process the ideas presented in a section
- Try activities out in your classroom
- Reflect on and discuss the outcomes of your lessons
- Read additional resources as needed

Even if you work independently on this program, time spent discussing your experiences with a colleague will be invaluable. In responding to your colleague's feedback and questions, you will clarify and further refine your "take" on vocabulary instruction.

It is also worth noting that the vocabulary development activities in this book were designed to be successful with very little preparation. Ideally, your greatest time investment will be made thinking about the way the ready-made lessons and activities can best be adapted to your teaching environment.

How do I begin?

We know that the first step in effective lesson planning is pre-assessment: determining what our learners want to, need to, and already know. To plan our own professional development, we need to engage in this same process. Begin by thinking about your classes and, more specifically, how you teach vocabulary. Identify what is working well for you and your learners. Next, consider which aspects of your vocabulary teaching you'd like to enhance. Once you've identified your professional development goals, you will be better able to use this book to help achieve them.

TASK: Keep a vocabulary teaching diary over a period of four or five class sessions. After each class, write the number of new words you introduced that day and why, as well as the techniques you used to teach them (e.g., visuals, worksheets, dictionary definitions, etc.). Also indicate whether learners retained the new vocabulary by the end of the lesson.

REFLECTION: Use the entries in your teaching diary to think about your answers to these questions:

1. What is your vocabulary teaching style?
2. What is working well for your learners? For you?
3. What changes, if any, would you like to make in your vocabulary instruction?
4. Based on your answers to 1–3, which sections of this book do you want to look at first?

Ready, set… jump!

My enthusiasm for professional development may seem a bit over the top to some. Each time I begin a professional development adventure, I thrill at the anticipation of chewing on new ideas. I puff up at the thought that I will be validated in what I do. And I am overcome by waves of fear and loathing: *What if everything I thought I knew—I don't? I don't have time to rethink everything now! What if the people I'm working with are shocked that I didn't know this all before?* I share these thoughts to assure you that I do understand what it takes to leap into the lesser known and think about creating change. The bottom line for us all is that as educators we owe it to ourselves and our learners to take these excursions beyond our comfort zone. When you think about it, the professional development process is less like a leap into the void than it is like a bungee jump—it brings us back up to where we were, in an exhilarated and energized state, breathlessly ready to jump again.

As you participate in this professional development program, you can access additional resources at www.oup.com/elt/teacher/opd, or feel free to email me at OPDteam.us@oup.com with your questions or comments.

Onward!

Jyme

Jayme Adelson-Goldstein

Most language learning methods recognize that there are words non-native speakers need in order to survive in a native-speaker environment: words they need to succeed academically, to succeed in the workplace, and to participate as members of the community. Most late twentieth-century instruction relied on the direct instruction of a limited number of these key words and assumed learners would acquire the remaining vocabulary words through incidental learning—for example, by encountering new words through listening or reading. Twenty-first-century research, however, points to the issues that arise when we rely on incidental learning. Many adult immigrant learners who do not have strong literacy skills cannot read extensively enough to develop the kind of active vocabulary they need for more than low-level communication. Even learners with more developed literacy skills do not know how to learn the vocabulary they encounter. A combination of direct instruction of vocabulary and explicit practice of vocabulary learning strategies learners apply outside the classroom is now seen as critical to learners' successful vocabulary acquisition.

Simply understanding that direct vocabulary instruction remains an important part of our curriculum does not answer the question at the heart of vocabulary instruction: Which words should be taught? In their 1997 article "Vocabulary Size, Text Coverage and Word Lists," Paul Nation and Robert Waring suggest considering three things: the number of words in English, the number of words native English speakers know, and the number of words needed to do what English language users need to do.[2]

How many words are there in English?

If you'd like to create a lively discussion, simply ask a couple of linguists, "How many words are there in English?" The discussion will probably begin with a debate over which words to count. The word *run*, for example, has more than 30 meanings in its verb form.[3] The noun form has at least 12 meanings. There are three inflections (*runs, ran, running*), and numerous derivations (*runner, run off, run in*, etc.). For just this reason, some linguists put the number of English words at around 1 million, a number based on the more than half-million word forms in *The Oxford English Dictionary* (the *OED*) and the approximately half-million scientific and technical terms not yet catalogued. More and more, however, researchers choose to count word families—a grouping of words that includes a head word, all that word's inflected forms and its transparent derivations.

Currently, the conservative estimate is that there are 54,000 word families in English.[4]

How many words can we expect non-native speakers to acquire? To determine that number, we can look at the number of words native speakers actually use. College-educated native English speakers may have an overall vocabulary of approximately 20,000 word families (or about 100,000 words). This number takes into account both active vocabulary (the words produced, listened for, and read in daily life) and receptive or passive vocabulary (words recognized but not actively used).

> **REFLECTION:** Using a thesaurus, read through the list of synonyms and antonyms for a word you know. Select one word from the list, that you never use. Reflect on why this word isn't in your active vocabulary.

Which words do we use most often?

If we focus on the college-educated native speaker's active vocabulary of between 6,000 and 7,000 word families (perhaps 10,000 words), we have a number that has decreased substantially from our initial discussion of 54,000 word families/1 million words. Still, 10,000 is a fairly daunting number. A high-intermediate or advanced-level ESL learner, with a strong academic background and a strong basic vocabulary, may be in a position to start tackling 6,000 to 7,000 word families inside and outside the classroom.[5] For our beginning-level and low-intermediate-level learners, however, we need to prioritize our vocabulary instruction by determining which words will allow them to do the things they need to do. Research has shown that a basic vocabulary of about 2,000 words comprises about 87 percent of what native speakers read, and about 90 percent of their conversations.[6] We can find versions of these 2000 words on word lists based on corpora of written and spoken language. These lists are often organized by the frequency of the word within the selected corpus. (A corpus is a set of language examples taken from one language's texts or speech; a typical corpus contains millions of items and is used to show the frequency of specific items in that language.) Some of the more popular beginning-level lists are West's 1953 General Service word list (GSL) and its 1995 revision by Bauer, as well as the Dolch (1936) and Fry (2004) reading vocabulary lists. Word lists for higher-level learners may be based on Xue and Nation's university word list (1984), or the academic word list (AWL) that Coxhead published in 2000.[7] Because the

GSL and the AWL include frequency rankings, they can help instructors (and curriculum writers) quickly determine the sequence of vocabulary instruction in a beginning, intermediate, or advanced class.

Top 5 words in the GSL		
GSL Ranking	Word	Frequency number*
1	the	69,975
2	be	39,175
3	of	36,432
4	and	28,872
5	a	26,800

*The frequency number represents the number of occurrences of that word and its related forms in the 1,000,000 words of the Brown corpus.

What else should I consider when selecting words to teach?

When choosing which words to teach, it's important to analyze how difficult a word may be to learn. Words that are high frequency and more difficult should be presented and practiced in class. Words that are easy to learn can be made part of incidental learning in a listening or reading activity or assigned in a take-home vocabulary list. Batia Laufer (2006) identifies several kinds of words that may be more difficult for learners, among which are words that have no equivalent in the learner's first language, (e.g. Hebrew has no word for *cozy*) or words that are false cognates (e.g. *embarrassed* in English and *embarazado*, "pregnant," in Spanish).[8]

Still, word lists and word difficulty are only part of the story. When planning communicative, student-centered lessons, we create lesson objectives that match our learners' workplace, academic, and life skill needs. The vocabulary we teach should support those objectives.

A picture dictionary is very useful for determining beginning- and low-intermediate-level learners' vocabulary needs. Give pairs of learners a picture dictionary and a worksheet and have them look through the pages to find ten topics they agree they need to learn. Learners write their top ten topics and the corresponding page numbers in a chart like the following:

Topic	Page	Topic	Page
1.		6.	
2.		7.	
3.		8.	
4.		9.	
5.		10.	

Of course, your learners will want to name more than ten topics. You can help them prioritize by having them list all the topics and page numbers they think are most important for them and then asking them to go back and choose their top ten. Another way to help limit the scope of the activity is to have learners look through only one unit at a time and list their top three topics. For example, in the *OPD*, you might have learners look through the unit on food (*OPD* Unit 4, pages 66–85) and select from these topics:

- Back from the Market
- Fruit
- Vegetables
- Meat and Poultry
- Seafood and Deli
- A Grocery Store
- Containers and Packaging
- Weights and Measurements
- Food Preparation and Safety
- Kitchen Utensils
- Fast Food Restaurant
- A Coffee Shop Menu
- A Restaurant
- The Farmers' Market

It may be that your learners use their own community grocery stores and therefore would not select grocery store or food packaging as high-priority topics. They might, however, want to learn the vocabulary for food preparation or kitchen utensils because of their needs in the workplace. This kind of "check in" with learners ensures that your curriculum matches their needs and goals. This in turn increases learners' motivation and their persistence.

In answer to the question of which words we should teach, we know that we have to consider the words on the frequency word lists, the words that students will struggle with if we don't teach them in class, and, most importantly, the words that learners need to complete the communication tasks in their daily lives.

TASK: Analyze a reading passage from your ESL textbook to determine the frequency of the top five GSL words within the passage. Next, identify which words in the passage would be difficult for your students to learn and which of those words would be necessary to support a meaningful communication task.

REFLECTION: How could you use the information from your analysis to inform your vocabulary teaching?

What is a vocabulary learning strategy?

Vocabulary learning strategies (VLS) are the tactics that native and non-native speakers use to identify the meaning of new words when they encounter them and to retain the meaning of those new words once they are understood.

Research has shown that no one vocabulary learning strategy works best for all learners. In fact, learners often work with a variety of strategies at the same time. A focus on the use of these strategies, both inside and outside the classroom, recognizes the important role learners play in their own vocabulary development. No matter how well we plan our lessons and prioritize word lists, ESL students cannot rely on the time spent within a classroom's four walls to provide them with the active English vocabulary they need. Learners must actively pursue new words in their daily lives, and explicit instruction in vocabulary learning strategies can help them do so successfully.

How many types of VLS are there?

Norbert Schmitt (1997) lists 58 different types of VLS which he divides into five groups:[9]

- **Determination strategies** allow learners to independently determine the meaning of a word when they first encounter it.

- **Social strategies** are employed by learners in conjunction with teachers, classmates, and others to get the meaning of or build retention of new words.

- **Mnemonic strategies** are associative tactics that learners use to remember words.

- **Cognitive strategies** involve studying or mechanically working with the target vocabulary.

- **Metacognitive strategies** are learner-generated strategies to analyze, monitor, and improve the learner's vocabulary learning process.

It's important to incorporate strategies from all five groups in our lessons to ensure that learners work with the strategy that works best for them. For example if students encounter the word *peaceful* in a reading, they could look up the word (determination strategy) or ask you or their classmates for the meaning (social strategy). Depending on their level, you could model more determination strategies by having them identify the root word and name the suffix. They could name other words they know with the same suffix (e.g., *careful*, *beautiful*, *helpful*). They could then work with different types of strategies to help them move the word deeper into their memory. For example, employing a mnemonic strategy, you might ask them to think of a beautiful, quiet, peaceful place and have them picture the word and the place in their mind. Similarly, they could also make a list of places and categorize them as *peaceful* or *not peaceful/ hectic*. These mnemonic strategies involve complex mental processing and make it much more likely that the new word will be remembered. Cognitive strategies, such as completing workbook substitution exercises or labeling pictures with target vocabulary, also help learners recall new words by providing repeated exposure to the new words and their meaning. When we have learners follow up the workbook or labeling exercise by testing themselves on the new words (metacognitive strategy) or working with a partner to make new sentences using the target vocabulary (cognitive and social strategies) we increase the likelihood of vocabulary retention.

How do I teach VLS?

One way to approach VLS instruction is to start by emphasizing a few strategies your learners already use (e.g., looking up words in a bilingual dictionary or repeating and memorizing lists of words) and adding three to five more strategies during the course.

Once you've determined the strategies you will focus on, you need to demonstrate how they're used and give students the opportunity to practice using them. For example, I demonstrate the social strategy of asking for the meaning of a word by having a learner write a sentence in his or her language on the board. I then try to read the sentence and ask the class about the words I don't understand. *Hmm. I don't know what this means. Do you know what this means? Do you know the definition? What does it mean?* When someone in the class gives me a definition, I model ways of clarifying meaning by repeating and restating. *So, it's a fruit? A melon?* Sometimes I draw a simple picture to verify my understanding. I then give a very brief explanation of the strategy I've demonstrated. *Sometimes you don't understand a word, but your friend knows the word. You can ask each other, What does that mean? Do you know what … means?*

To provide practice with this social strategy I write five to 12 words from the lesson on the board. (Some or all of the words may be new, target vocabulary.) First, students work independently and list those words from the board that they already know. They then ask their group members for the meaning of any unknown words. If some words have a group stumped, a group representative can visit other groups to see if they know the word. If there are still words that no one in the class knows when time is called, learners can look up those words in the *OPD*, a learner's dictionary, or a bilingual dictionary. Once all the words have been defined by the class, learners can add the new words and their meanings to their vocabulary notebooks.

To internalize a strategy, learners have to practice it repeatedly, both in and out of class. If a student says, "Teacher, I don't understand *empty*," I encourage him or her to ask someone in the class, "What does *empty* mean?" In an intermediate-level class, we first practice the language for polite interrupting and role play different situations where one might ask for the meaning of a word (in a doctor's office, at the workplace, or at a teacher conference). I then give learners the assignment of bringing in words they've learned during conversations outside the classroom. I ask them to start a conversation in English during everyday situations (at the market, in the laundromat) using small talk techniques. When they hear an unknown words, they are to interrupt politely and ask for the meaning of the word.

To complete the assignment, learners turn in index cards with the following information:

New word	Meaning

I spoke with a <u>native speaker / non-native speaker</u>.

I <u>knew / did not know</u> the speaker.

It was <u>easy / a little difficult / very difficult</u> to understand the speaker.

Which VLS should I teach first?

The following list of 20 strategies, adapted from a chart in Norbert Schmitt's *Vocabulary in Language Teaching* (2000), is a good starting point for thinking about which VLS to include in your classes. In order for learners to acquire a strategy, you'll need to demonstrate it, verify learners' comprehension of how to use it, and provide lots of in-class practice so that students can apply it.

To determine the meanings of words, learners can

- ask classmates for meaning.
- use a monolingual dictionary.
- use a bilingual dictionary or electronic dictionary.
- use a computer program.
- analyze new words to determine their parts of speech.
- analyze the affixes and roots of new words.
- guess meaning from textual or situational context.
- ask the teacher for a synonym or definition.

To move words into their active vocabulary, learners can

- categorize/group words in order to study them.
- look for cognates.
- test themselves.
- use flash cards.
- repeat the new words.
- watch TV shows in English.
- affix word labels to objects around the home.
- connect words to personal experiences.
- keep a vocabulary notebook.
- use imagery to connect new words with meaning.
- say new words aloud.
- connect physical actions to words when studying.

REFLECTION: Which of the strategies above do you personally use when learning new words? Which do you use most often? Which do your learners use? Why?

What are the stages of a typical communicative lesson?

A communicative lesson is structured around a meaningful language objective that reflects the learners' needs. The lesson includes a communication task that learners will be able to accomplish at the end of the lesson, such as requesting or giving the price of an item in a store or interpreting apartment ads in order to determine which apartments to see.

To achieve this objective, a communicative lesson takes learners through a progression of stages. Although lesson plans can and should vary based on the needs, interests, backgrounds, and prior knowledge of the learners, a typical communicative lesson plan includes the following stages.

Warm-up / Review

Activities in this stage generally make use of content and language that learners already know, that activate their prior knowledge of the lesson topic, and that engage them with their classmates in a way that builds classroom community. In many adult ESL programs—where learners find themselves at the mercy of public transportation or uncooperative work schedules—learners will often miss the warm-up activities. For this reason, warm-up and review activities should be considered helpful, but not essential, to the learners' success during the rest of the lesson.

Introduction

The main goal of the introduction stage of the communicative lesson is to focus learners on the lesson objective and its relevance to their goals outside the classroom.

Presentation and comprehension check

At this stage, learners are exposed to the new information—target vocabulary, new grammar, functional phrases, dialogue patterns, or cultural information—they will need to accomplish the lesson objective. After presenting the information, it's critical to check the learners' comprehension of the new material.

Guided practice

This stage of the lesson provides learners with opportunities to work with the new information that was presented. Guided practice activities aim to increase learners' retention of new material as well as their accuracy in producing this material, both orally and in writing. In general, guided practice activities tend to emphasize accuracy more than fluency.

Communicative practice

The true test of a lesson's success is whether the learners can master the communication task set for them in the objective. Many times the communicative practice stage of the lesson allows you to see whether learners have the ability to master the task—for example, by role-playing returning an item to the store, or by responding to survey questions that could be asked in a job interview. Communicative-practice activities include surveys, interviews, role-plays, problem-solving activities, and discussions. These types of activities ask learners to use the language they've learned in the lesson as well as previously learned language. While guided practice develops learners' accuracy, communicative practice tasks develop their fluency and ownership of the language.

Evaluation

In this stage of the lesson we may be testing any of the following:

- Have learners attained the lesson objective? (e.g., *Learners will be able to return an item to the store.*)

- Can they identify and use the target vocabulary? (e.g., *torn, too small, stained.*)

- Can they accurately use the grammar structures needed to achieve the objective? (e.g., *It's stained. They're torn.*)

In some lessons, activities in the communicative practice or application stages may provide you with opportunities to evaluate your learners' abilities. But even when these types of evaluation activities occur in a lesson, you may also want to give learners a short pen-and-paper quiz on the lesson's grammar, vocabulary, or both to help them keep track of their progress in these areas.

Application

This stage of the lesson offers learners opportunities to apply lesson content to real-life situations, such as filling in a form, listening for specific information from authentic (or authentic-sounding) recordings, or using a map to ask for and give directions.

How do I choose the vocabulary for a communicative lesson?

Once you have decided on a lesson objective, it's possible to determine which grammar structures and which vocabulary words are needed to achieve that objective. It's important to be aware that learners may have prior knowledge of the lesson content, vocabulary and grammar structures. Finding out what learners already know will help you target instruction to their needs. To get a better understanding of your learners' prior vocabulary knowledge, you may want to conduct pre-assessment activities like the following:

Word survey

A word survey is an effective pre-assessment tool suitable for strong high-beginning or low-intermediate learners.

1. Have learners write the first ten words on the picture dictionary page in the first column of a chart like the one below.

2. For each word, learners check the column that is true for them.

Word or phrase	First time I've seen it	Use it	Want to add it	Don't need it

Page 36 of this *Handbook* includes a full-sized word survey worksheet you can use with your learners.

Pictures to words

This pre-assessment activity is good for beginning-level learners because of its visual focus. In this example, learners focus on pictures of weather conditions from the *OPD* page on weather (page 13, below).

1. Ask learners to look at the pictures.

2. Have them name the weather conditions they know.

3. Tell learners to write the numbers of the words they want to learn.

How can I help students learn the words they need?

We know that learners play an important role in their own vocabulary development, but so do we! As discussed in the last section, instructors need to explicitly teach both key vocabulary and vocabulary learning strategies (VLS).

But teaching key vocabulary and VLS isn't enough. Vocabulary instruction needs to be integrated in a meaningful way throughout the lesson with an awareness of the stages of vocabulary development:

- Comprehension
- Retention
- Production
- Recognition out of the original context
- Ownership

Helping our learners become aware of these stages helps them chart their progress as they expand their vocabulary inside the classroom. This in turn boosts their confidence in using and expanding their vocabulary outside of the classroom as well.

What happens in each stage of vocabulary development?

One of the best ways to understand the stages of vocabulary development is to look at an example. Recently I learned the word *retronym*. My encounter with this word took me through the five stages of vocabulary development:

I first saw the word *retronym* on a Web site listing words added to the English language in 2006. By analyzing the word, I assumed it had something to do with word usage. To verify my **comprehension,** I looked it up. Thanks to the following comprehensible input (a definition and an example), I soon understood the word very well.

retronym

retronym *n* a word or phrase created because an existing term that was once used alone needs to be distinguished from a term referring to a new development, as *acoustic guitar* in contrast to *electric guitar*

Origins 1980: *retro-* + *-onym*

While it would have been possible to move down the list skimming other new words, retronym seemed like it would be useful, so I made an effort to remember it. To ensure **retention**, I repeated it to myself a few times, and made a mental association with the idea of retrofitting. I then wrote the word on a sticky note and put it on my computer monitor.

Later that evening I used the term when I spoke to a colleague. (I admit that saying the word out loud gave me a little thrill, but then **production** of new language can do that to a person.)

When I saw the word in a Web article several days later, I was delighted. My **recognition** of the word out of the original context, made me start thinking about retronyms all over again. As I ruminated on what retronyms meant to the development of language, I asked myself, *Are retronyms a reflection of specialization, or of having more things to name? Are they easier to get into the language than a completely new word?* In going beyond merely remembering or saying the word, I was now using it to think critically about language. Clearly, I had taken **ownership** of this word.

As you can see, these five stages of vocabulary development played an important role in my progress from comprehension to ownership. However, while my vocabulary encounter followed the sequence above, I could just as easily have seen the word in a different context before I produced it, or (because of my language level) thought about the ideas associated with the word before ever seeing it in a different context.

How do the stages of vocabulary development fit into a communicative lesson?

The stages of vocabulary development work in conjunction with the stages of a communicative lesson, but it is helpful to consider how these two sets of stages overlap.

Communicative lesson	Vocabulary development
Presentation	Comprehension
Comprehension check	
Guided practice	Retention, production
Communicative practice	Production, ownership
Evaluation	Retention, production
Application	Ownership, recognition

Ensuring comprehension

During the presentation, learners are at the comprehension stage of vocabulary development. Remember that while learners are clear on the meaning of the target language you are presenting, they may not be ready to produce new words. To ensure that learners understand the target vocabulary, use comprehensible input such as visuals, realia, media, and learner experiences to present new words.

It's appropriate to conduct nonverbal comprehension checks (in which learners respond with *yes/no/not sure* cards or *a/b/c/d* cards for multiple choice questions) as well as verbal comprehension checks (asking *yes/no, or,* and *wh-* questions).

Answer cards are a nonverbal way to check learners' comprehension of the language they'll be asked to produce in the practice stages of the lesson.

From retention to production

Once learners have shown they understand the target vocabulary, it's critical to build their retention of the new words and give them opportunities to practice producing them. Guided practice activities are an ideal way to increase learners' exposure to the target vocabulary and provide oral and written practice in a controlled setting. Each time learners use the new word in a simple listen-and-point activity or a conversation substitution drill (see page 21), the word goes deeper into memory.

Recognizing the vocabulary out of context

It is also possible during the guided practice stage to give learners opportunities to recognize a word out of its original context. Using workbooks with images or narratives different from those used to present the new language creates a new context in which learners can recognize the target word.

Production leading to ownership

In many cases, communicative practice and application activities in the lesson are where learners demonstrate their ownership of the new language. Interactive activities such as an information gap (see page 29) allow learners to produce target vocabulary in a meaningful exchange, building their fluency with the new words. Discussions or problem-solving activities allow learners to use the new words to express their opinions and reasoning. For example, a problem-solving scenario about someone who gets caught in bad weather on the way to a job interview, would allow learners to use the weather words from the lesson as part of their statement of the problem and in their ideas for solutions to the problem.

Assessing vocabulary development

In the communicative lesson, learners are evaluated on their achievement of the lesson objective. Evaluation activities can assess learners' recall of the target vocabulary as well as their ability to produce the target words orally or in writing. Matching exercises, multiple choice sentence completion, and role plays are just some of the activities that allow learners to demonstrate how well they've acquired the new language.

It's important to remember that it's not at all uncommon for learners to skip around the stages. While the comprehension stage of vocabulary development must come first if learners are going to work with words they understand, it's possible to work on recognition before production or vice versa. An intermediate learner may be much more likely to use new words, but struggle when hearing them or reading them out of context. A beginner may be able to recognize the new words in different contexts, but not be ready to produce them. The key is to be aware of the different stages of vocabulary development and provide enough practice with the lesson's target vocabulary that learners are able to move beyond classroom comprehension toward remembering, recognizing, using, and owning the new words.

Teaching Vocabulary within the Communicative Lesson

Integrating the stages of vocabulary development within the lesson

As shown in the weather lesson below, the stages of vocabulary development integrate naturally into a communicative lesson. Each stage of a lesson can include one or more stages of vocabulary development.

Level: High Beginning	**Topic:** Weather	**OPD:** p.13

Objective: Learners will be able to ask for and give local and national weather conditions.	**Vocabulary:** Weather conditions and temperatures.	**Grammar focus:** Simple tenses of *be*: present, past, future

Warm-up / Review: Draw an outline of the US on the board and put a numbered list of cities such as Chicago, Denver, New York, etc., next to the map. Have learners say or guess where the cities are located. Have them write each city's number on the map.

Introduction: Have learners brainstorm weather words they know. Write the words on the board. Tell learners the lesson objective.

Presentation: Give a weather report based on the *OPD* weather map. Use vocabulary items 1–12 as well as words learners identified in the introduction activity: *It's raining in Chicago. It's snowing in New York.*

Comprehension check: Ask *yes/no* questions about the weather map (*Is it raining in Chicago?*) and have learners respond with answer cards.

Guided practice: Have learners organize weather words into categories (good weather / bad weather); conduct peer dictation; have learners do the exercises on *Workbook* page 13; conduct pair practice using the model conversation at the bottom of *OPD* page 13.

Communicative practice: Have pairs ask and answer questions about weather conditions using actual weather maps from the Internet or a newspaper.

Evaluation: Monitor the communicative practice and make note of language issues for future lessons.

Application: Have learners listen to or watch a weather report (an actual one or one from the *OPD Multilevel Listening* program in the *OPD Lesson Plans*) and listen for local and national weather conditions.

Closing: Play tic-tac-toe with weather vocabulary. Place nine different weather symbols or temperatures on the tic-tac-toe grid. Team X and Team O take turns selecting a square on the grid and answering questions such as *What's the weather like in Tampa, Florida?*

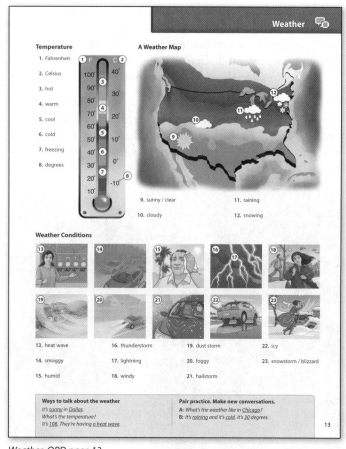

Weather, OPD page 13

Introduction and presentation

In the sample lesson, learners' comprehension of the target language is increased through a brainstorming activity that taps prior knowledge and through the use of the weather map and illustrations on the *OPD* page. Using the weather map on the board foreshadows the communicative task learners will do later in the lesson.

Presenting the target language in context (It's raining in Chicago) allows learners to hear a model of the language that they'll later be producing.

Guided practice

In the sample lesson, a categorizing activity gives learners who are ready to produce the new words a chance to do so, while those who are not ready get more exposure to the words. It's good to point out to learners that categorizing is an effective vocabulary learning strategy. The peer dictation activity gives learners speaking and listening practice, while the workbook exercises offer reading and writing practice. The controlled conversation practice prepares learners for the communicative task to come.

A peer dictation activity allows learners to produce and listen for the new words while employing critical clarification strategies (Please spell that. Did you say rain or raining?).

Communicative practice

Learners in the sample lesson begin to own the language as they engage in an authentic, meaningful conversation about actual weather maps.

Providing level-appropriate prompts for the weather map conversations means learners at all levels can have authentic exchanges using the target language.

Application

The sample lesson's application activity—listening for specific weather information—expands the learners' recognition of the vocabulary out of its original context.

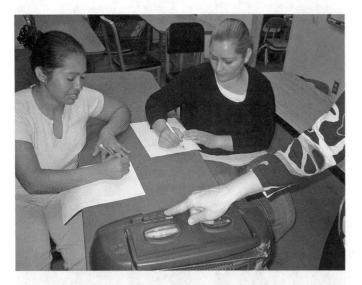

Integrating VLS into the lesson

Along with the stages of vocabulary development, direct instruction of the vocabulary learning strategies that learners employ within these stages is also valuable. For example, in the introduction, you can ask learners to open their picture dictionaries and look up words their classmates named that they don't know (a determination strategy). Or, as learners categorize the weather conditions, you can tell them they're practicing a vocabulary learning strategy they may want to use with other new words they learn.

> **REFLECTION:** Look at the lesson on page 14. Which vocabulary learning strategies are being employed in the lesson? How would you call your learners' attention to these strategies?

Using multilevel strategies for vocabulary instruction

As the sample lesson on page 14 demonstrates, the integration of vocabulary development into a beginning-level communicative lesson can be fairly seamless. The challenges occur when the vocabulary list is more abstract (because it may take longer to make these new words comprehensible) or when the class is multilevel

and learners have a spectrum of vocabulary needs. The multilevel strategies presented next make it possible to effectively address both of these challenges.

Identifying level-specific objectives

The principles of multilevel instruction include creating level-specific objectives linked to a single theme. Ideally, there are no more than three objectives: one each for the lower, middle, and higher levels in a class. In practice, this may involve grouping two levels of learners together; for example, in a class with literacy-level learners, low beginners, high beginners, and low-intermediate learners, the low and high beginners may constitute the mid-level group, or the literacy learners and low beginners may form the lower-level group. The three leveled objectives below would work for a class of low-beginning, high-beginning and low-intermediate learners focusing on the theme of weather.

- **Low beginner:** Identify common weather conditions
- **High beginner:** Ask for and give local weather conditions
- **Low intermediate:** Listen for national weather conditions and emergencies

The support vocabulary associated with these objectives expands from basic weather conditions (for the lower-level group) to weather emergencies (for the higher-level group). In the presentation stage of this lesson, using visuals and other comprehensible input, the vocabulary for all levels can be made comprehensible across levels. In the practice stage, however, learners would only practice the words needed to achieve their objectives.

In some cases, rather than presenting higher-level vocabulary to the whole group, you may want higher-level learners to work together on their vocabulary while other groups begin their practice tasks. The higher-level learners can go over the vocabulary list for their levels objective and, after collaboratively defining the words they know, look up those they don't.

> **TASK:** List the vocabulary higher-level learners would need to achieve their objective: *Listen for national weather conditions and emergencies.* Then list the types of visuals or items you would use to make the vocabulary comprehensible across all levels in the class.

Using leveled questions

In multilevel instruction, using different types of questions make it possible to check whether learners at different levels comprehend the new, target vocabulary that supports their level's objective. These leveled questions can also be used to ensure comprehension of the review vocabulary needed for the mid- and higher-level objectives. The types of questions that can be used effectively to check comprehension of new language are nonverbal commands, *yes/no* questions, and *or* questions. To check comprehension of review language, use *or* questions, *wh-* questions, and leading statements. For example, during the comprehension check in the sample weather lesson, you could ask these types of comprehension questions:

Level	Question for reviewed language	Command/Question for new language
Lower-level	N/A	(show thermometer) Point to 70°. (show picture) *Is it raining?*
Mid-level	(show thermometer) *Is this 70° or 17°?*	*Is it raining in New York? Is 70° hot?*
Higher-level	*What type of weather are we having today? When the sun is out and it's 80°, the weather is…*	*Do tornadoes occur in the Midwest? Do they happen in blizzards or in thunderstorms?*

Using simultaneous same-level activities

One of the pitfalls for new multilevel instructors is trying to teach three separate classes rather than using group work to help learners achieve their objectives. Simultaneous, same-level guided practice activities ensure that learners at all levels work on retaining and producing the language needed to achieve their level-specific objectives. In the sample weather lesson, for example, learners at each level could do a peer dictation using the words appropriate to their specific objective. At the higher levels, this may mean learners dictate sentences with more advanced grammar structures.

Workbooks are especially useful for multilevel practice. When learners spend time completing exercises in their level-specific workbooks, they are working with vocabulary that will help them achieve their level-specific objective. Workbooks are also an important "wait time" tool learners can use when they've completed an activity, but their classmates have not.

Developing mixed-level activities

When learners work in mixed-level groups, they use language in a more authentic situation: communicating in a group with diverse abilities and needs. Assigning different roles or tasks to learners during practice activities allows them to work together while still working toward their various level objectives. For example, in the weather lesson's peer dictation activity, higher-level learners can dictate words to lower-level learners, giving the higher-level learners the opportunity to work on their pronunciation. In a listening activity such as the one from the sample weather lesson, each level could listen for different information in a weather report like the one below from the *OPD Multilevel Listening* program.

Reporter: The hot, humid weather continues in the Midwest, with severe thunderstorms expected across Missouri. There is a tornado watch for Kansas City from 6:00 p.m. to midnight. Currently, Kansas City is 80°.

Learners could be asked to listen for the following information:

- **Lower-level learners:** Is it hot or cold? Is it 80° or 18°?

- **Mid-level learners:** What's the weather like in the Midwest? What's the temperature in Kansas City?

- **Higher-level learners:** What's the weather emergency? Where's the weather emergency? When should people stay alert?

Communicative practice activities that lend themselves to mixed-level task and role assignments include role plays, information exchanges, and team projects such as posters or oral reports.

> **REFLECTION:** In terms of vocabulary development, what are the benefits to learners working in mixed-level groups? What are the challenges? How would you address these challenges?

The ideal communicative lesson allows learners to work towards the completion of a communication task while using an integrated set of skills (listening, speaking, reading, and writing) and practicing target grammar and vocabulary. Lesson planning is essential to ensuring that learners move successfully through each stage and achieve the lesson objective. And while lesson planning can be a daunting task, with a collection of ready-made teaching tools such as texts and pictures, as well as a repertoire of 10 to 15 instructional activities, lesson planning can become a process of selection that allows you to spend less time on the mechanics of the lesson and more time on the art of teaching.

A picture dictionary is one of the most flexible resources for language instruction. Unlike a textbook, it is not sequential, so a class lesson can be organized around the learners' needs. Because it is arranged by topics within themes, it can serve as the foundation for beginning-level, intermediate-level, and multilevel instruction. Almost any page of a picture dictionary may be used as the basis for warm-up, review, introduction, presentation, practice, application, and evaluation activities. And because a picture dictionary provides so many opportunities for vocabulary development, using this type of resource ensures that effective vocabulary instruction will be integrated into a lesson.

The ideas below illustrate some of the ways in which a picture dictionary can support instruction. Depending on the lesson topic, it can also prepare learners for authentic listening and speaking tasks, communicative writing, and life-skill reading.

How do I use a picture dictionary in the warm-up / review stage of the lesson?

To conduct a simple ten-minute warm-up activity using a picture dictionary:

1. Select a page with a scene or a set of pictures that relate to the current lesson, e.g., the *OPD* page on shopping (page 27, right).

2. On the board, write three true sentences and three false sentences about the scene or pictures. For example, using the pictures from the *OPD* page on shopping (page 27, right):

    1. There are five people in these pictures. (T)
    2. A woman is buying a lamp. (T)
    3. She's paying with a credit card. (F)
    4. The male customer is giving the clerk a receipt. (F)
    5. He's writing a check. (F)
    6. The male customer is exchanging a lamp. (T)

3. Give learners 15–30 seconds to study the scene or pictures and then have them close their books.

4. Reveal the first sentence on the board and get class consensus on whether the sentence is true or false. Continue the process with all six sentences.

5. Invite learners to come to the board to revise the false sentences to make them true. Encourage learners to give respectful feedback to each other, and have them look in their picture dictionaries to check their work.

Here are three more strategies for previewing/reviewing using a picture dictionary:

- Project an overhead transparency of a picture dictionary page and have learners call out all the words they see in the illustrations.

- Write scrambled sentences on the board that relate to the illustrations on a dictionary page. Have learners look in their picture dictionaries in order to unscramble the sentences.

- Select two or three previously studied topics that are related to the lesson and put their page numbers on the board. Have learners select five words from any of the pages to add to their vocabulary notebooks (see page 33.)

REFLECTION: What are some ways you could adapt these warm-up/review activities for learners with limited literacy skills?

G. buy / pay for

H. return

I. exchange

Shopping, OPD page 27

How do I use a picture dictionary to introduce the lesson?

Introducing new language or content with visuals is an effective way to get the learners' attention, support comprehension, and make connections between the lesson and the real world.

In a lesson on renting an apartment, for example, you could start by showing the housing ads from the *OPD* page on finding a home (page 48, right) and asking learners to tell you as much as they can about the apartments in the ads.

You could also introduce the topic by showing learners the pictures of the apartment buildings from the *OPD* pages on apartments (pages 50 and 51, below) and asking them where they'd look for an apartment.

Finding a Home, OPD *page 48*

Apartments, OPD *page 50*

Apartments, OPD *page 51*

How do I use a picture dictionary to present and check comprehension of the lesson?

While there are as many ways to present new information as there are teachers to present it, the strategies below form the basis of a successful presentation repertoire:

- Tell a story using pictures and real objects (realia)
- Ask questions about pictures or realia
- Act out a sequence (such as making a phone call)
- Act out a conversation alone or with learners
- Describe the new concepts and language

Imagine that your lesson objective is that learners will be able to ask an apartment manager questions about renting an apartment. First, learners have to understand the rental process, and then they need to be able to ask the appropriate questions. You could begin by telling a story about the sequence of renting an apartment, using the illustrations on the *OPD* page on finding a home (page 48, below) and modeling the appropriate questions at each step. For example: *Maya Ramos is calling the manager about an apartment. She asks, "Is the apartment available?" and he says…*

Another presentation strategy is to act out the sequence with a higher-level learner serving as the manager.

You: Hi, I'm calling about the apartment. Is it available?

Student: Yes, it is.

Note that it's best if the learner is only responsible for responding to the questions rather than asking them.

After presenting new information, it's critical to check your learners' comprehension of the new material. To check learners' understanding you can

- ask *yes/no* and *or* questions about the new information. *(Look at the ad for the apartment. Is it for a two-bedroom apartment? Can you call the manager in the morning or in the evening?)*
- provide a series of *true/false* statements about the lesson and have learners hold up *true/false* cards in response. *(The manager submits an application. The tenant moves in.)*
- make mistakes while performing a sequence you've already demonstrated, and ask students to correct you. *(T: Okay, first I call the manager. Then I sign the rental agreement. Ss: No, ask about the features! T: Oh, that's right.)*
- provide prompts (e.g., visual clues or definitions) and have learners number, circle, or write out the key words or phrases from the lesson based on your prompt. *(The paper I sign to rent an apartment is called a…)*

> **REFLECTION:** Think of a topic for which one presentation strategy would be more effective than another. Is that presentation strategy better for higher-level learners or for lower-level learners? Explain.

> **TASK:** Imagine you've just finished a presentation on the ways to pay for an item. Write a series of statements that learners could answer with *true/false* cards.

Renting an Apartment

A. **Call** the manager.

B. **Ask** about the features.

C. **Submit** an application.

D. **Sign** the rental agreement.

E. **Pay** the first and last month's rent.

F. **Move in**.

Finding a Home, OPD page 48

How do I use a picture dictionary for guided practice?

Some effective guided practice activities for picture dictionaries include listen and point activities, peer dictation activities, and substitution drills.

Listen and point

This is the simplest activity to set up in the classroom. The learners form pairs. Learner A (the "sender") names words from the picture dictionary word list and Learner B points to the corresponding image on the page. (This is an ideal mixed-level activity, as higher-level "senders" can work on pronunciation of the vocabulary while lower-level learners can respond nonverbally.)

Peer dictation

In a peer dictation activity, learners again work in pairs. Learner A (the "sender") works with the book open and selects a word from the page to dictate to Learner B, whose book is closed. When modeling this activity for the class, be sure to demonstrate and practice a clarification strategy such as *Is that spelled…?* or *Did you say…?* to give learners the communication tools they need to successfully complete the dictation.

Both listen and point and peer dictation activities can be done in groups rather than pairs, with one learner calling out or dictating words to a small group of learners who point to or write what they hear. Each group member can take a turn being the "expert" sender. To narrow the scope of the words to be practiced, give the senders specific words to dictate, for example, *Senders, please dictate words one through seven on dictionary page 46.*

Substitution drills

Another classic ESL activity is the substitution drill, in which learners replace one or more target vocabulary words in a sentence with other target vocabulary words, practicing the sentence pattern but changing the meaning of the sentence. The best of these drills are embedded in meaningful conversation and practice "chunks" of language in addition to the target vocabulary. For example, on the *OPD* page on money (page 26), learners practice using vocabulary (monetary amounts) and a question (*Do you have…?*) to achieve the lesson objective: being able to ask for change.

A: Do you have change for <u>a dollar</u>?

B: Sure. How about <u>two quarters</u> and <u>five dimes</u>?

A: Perfect!

We know that learners need a wide variety of guided-practice tasks to help them produce the new language accurately and recognize it out of the original context. Picture dictionary ancillary materials such as audio programs, workbooks, and picture cards are all excellent for expanding this type of practice.

How do I give learners meaningful communicative practice with a picture dictionary?

Communicative practice activities that work well with picture dictionaries include role-play activities, interviews, surveys, problem-solving activities, discussions, and "page travel" activities.

Role-play activities

A role play prompts a conversation between learners but does not script it. This means that learners are free to bring their own experiences and ideas to the activity, creating an authentic exchange. For example, in the *OPD* pages on describing clothing (pages 96–97), learners practice returning a purchase in order to complete the lesson objective. Having students role play this situation allows them to demonstrate their ability to use the target vocabulary (problems with clothing) in a real-life situation (returning an item).

A: Welcome to Shopmart. How may I help you?

B: <u>This sweater</u> is new, but it's <u>unraveling</u>.

A: I'm sorry. Would you like a refund?

Interviews and surveys

Interviews and surveys can also be used as communicative practice. When learners ask and answer questions that are relevant to them, they are engaging in meaningful communication. Note that if a *yes/no* question is used in a survey or interview, it should be followed with an expansion question to be sure that higher-level thinking is engaged (e.g., *Do you like to take care of children? Why or why not?*).

To use questions as communicative practice, learners can pair up and ask each other the questions, do round-robin interviews in small groups, or conduct a classroom survey asking five to ten people for their answers.

Problem-solving activities and discussions

In a lesson with a communicative reading or writing objective, such as *Read and demonstrate understanding of a story about local community projects*, whole class or small group discussions are excellent follow-up communicative-practice activities. These types of activities teach communication strategies such as building consensus and expressing disagreement, and encourage learners to express higher-level thinking.

When discussion questions require only a short answer, it is important to ask learners to explain the rationale for each response. See the three examples below from the *OPD* page on money (page 26):

1. Is it a good idea to lend money to a friend? Why or why not?

2. Is it better to carry a dollar or four quarters? Why?

3. Do you prefer dollar coins or dollar bills? Why?

Page travel

While role plays, interviews, surveys, problem-solving activities, and discussions are often found in core textbooks, a communicative practice activity that is exclusive to a picture dictionary is page travel. In this type of activity, learners use the new language from one topic to talk about what they see on a different topic page. For example, learners who have studied the adjectives of appearance on *OPD* page 32 can turn to any number of pages in the dictionary and talk about the appearance of the people in the pictures. To ensure that learners are communicating real information rather than simply naming items, provide prompts to help them tell a story about the page using all the English they have available to them.

There are, of course, hundreds of communicative-practice activities, and not all of them are based on speaking and listening. Literacy and writing activities that allow learners to interact with texts and write communicatively are extremely important for learners at all levels. While picture-dictionary topics can provide an entrée into these types of activities, learners need explicit instruction and guided and communicative practice in these skill areas.

How do I conduct evaluation activities with a picture dictionary?

An easy way to evaluate learners' retention and use of vocabulary is to project an overhead transparency of the picture dictionary page you have been using and place sticky notes to obscure any visible word lists. Have learners write as many of the words from the lesson as they can. This activity adapts very well to multilevel classes: low beginners can write the words depicted in the illustrations, high beginners can write simple sentences about the illustrations, and low-intermediate learners can write a series of sentences or a conversation based on the illustration.

Another evaluation option is to give definitions of the target vocabulary and have learners find the matching words in their picture dictionary word list, then write the corresponding numbers on their papers. (For example, for the words describing clothing on *OPD* pages 96–97, after learners hear *This is the size between large and small,* they write *3* for medium.) A variation of this activity for lower-level learners is to show a picture card. For higher-level learners you can give conversational cues (e.g., *These pants are large, but I need one size smaller. Please bring me a…*).

In addition to these types of informal evaluations, you may want to use a computer program to create customized multiple-choice tests or have learners self-test using interactive software that includes a testing component.

How do I use a picture dictionary at the application stage?

Along with offering opportunities to apply the lesson content to real-life situations, the application stage of the lesson also gives learners practice recognizing the target vocabulary out of the original context. Learners can tell or write a story about an illustration in the picture dictionary that relates to, but is not the same as, the page used in the lesson. For example, if the lesson objective is for learners to be able to ask for directions, and they have already worked with the page on directions and maps (*OPD* page 155), they could look with a partner at the *OPD* pages on places downtown (*OPD* pages 124–125) or city streets (*OPD* pages 126–127) and give directions to different places pictured there.

The application stage is also an excellent time to use components associated with a picture dictionary such as readers, activity books, or interactive software. See page 32 for ways to use these components.

How do I pull all of these elements together?

While a picture dictionary is an excellent resource for a communicative lesson, a sequential lesson plan is the foundation for effective teaching. Lesson planning books for picture dictionaries abound. When looking at a ready-made lesson, be sure to ask these questions as you plan how to adapt the lesson for your class:

- Do the objectives in this lesson match my learners' needs? Do the target vocabulary items support the objective? Does the target grammar structure support the objective?

- Is there a clear connection between the objective, presentation, practice, and evaluation?

- Are the practice activities suitable for my classroom environment? What additional materials do I need for these activities?

- Are grouping strategies varied throughout the lesson? Are there kinesthetic as well as verbal activities?

- How are learners made aware of target vocabulary and target grammar structures?

- How does the lesson prepare learners to complete the objective's communication task?

- Is there an evaluation activity that helps learners see their progress toward a goal?

- How long will it take for me to teach this lesson?

TASK: Review the clothing lesson plan to the right using the questions above and determine what you would add to or delete from the lesson plan.

REFLECTION: Would you want to teach this lesson? Why or why not?

Level: Low Beginning	**Topic:** Clothing	**OPD:** pp. 86–87
Objective: Students will be able to identify five to ten common clothing items	**Vocabulary:** Everyday clothes	**Grammar:** present continuous (*He's wearing…*)

Warm-up, review, and introduction:
- Show the *OPD* page on the overhead projector and have learners in groups or pairs list words they see.
- Elicit words from class and list on the board.
- State the objective and the rationale for the lesson.

Presentation:
- Tell a story about or talk about the *OPD* scene, being sure to use additional comprehensible input for target words that students need.
- Ask students to tell you which of the words from the story were from the warm-up and which were new.
- Write the new words on the board, including any target words that students didn't name.
- Tell the story again.

Comprehension check: Use answer cards for *yes/no* questions and ask *or* and short answer questions about the page.

Guided practice:
- Conduct a substitution drill: *He's wearing _____.*
- Have pairs do a peer dictation activity.
- Have pairs categorize clothing from the page into two groups, *At school* and *At home*.

Communicative practice: Have pairs play a grid game with clothing picture cards. Each cell in the grid has a name. Students take turns asking and answering the question *What's _____ wearing?* and placing the picture cards appropriately.

Evaluation: Have students look at their *OPDs* and cover the word lists. Have students independently write 5–10 of the words from the lesson.

Application:
- Conduct a problem-solving activity. Show the school topic page in the picture dictionary (pp. 188 to 189). Tell a story about a student who wears the wrong clothes to school.
- Write a language experience letter to the student giving him advice.

Closing: Conduct a chain drill—Teacher: *Lola has a skirt in her closet.* Student 1: *She has a skirt and jeans.* Student 2: *She has a skirt, jeans, and a sweater.*

The research and reality of the semantic set

Research has questioned the value of introducing new words in semantic sets (e.g., colors, patterns, tools, etc.) Learners in three semantic-set experiments took longer to learn related imaginary words than to learn pairs of unrelated imaginary words. The vocabulary learners in these research experiments were two sets of native English speakers learning imaginary words defined in English, and one set of Japanese speakers learning imaginary words defined in Japanese.[10]

As critically reflective professionals, we need to consider this research and how it affects our teaching and our learners. It certainly heightens our awareness of the confusion learners can face when learning related terms and points out that this confusion can make vocabulary acquisition take longer. Monolingual picture dictionaries are reference tools that, by and large, are organized by semantic sets in order to give learners a way of looking up words they recognize conceptually but don't yet know in English. As a teaching tool, a picture dictionary's semantic sets meet the life-skill needs of the adult learner who may have an immediate need to know the parts of a car, sections of a pay stub, places at school, or service industry job titles. Related vocabulary lists thus play an important role in helping beginning and intermediate learners function at their jobs, in their communities, and

in school settings. We also know that learners are able to use determination strategies and social strategies to assign meaning to essential new words before we teach them in class, and that much of our vocabulary work lies not in introducing brand-new terms within a semantic set but in giving learners practice with these words so that can remember, recognize, and use the words accurately and fluently.

There are a number of ways to incorporate the research findings into our teaching. The first is to provide as much of a mix as we can in our initial presentation of new vocabulary by using a story or picture story that goes beyond a list of related words. Another strategy is to teach high frequency words first within a semantic set and to avoid introducing antonyms together when possible, although we have to consider whether those antonyms are prone to being used together.

For example, in talking about weather conditions across the United States, learners will want to be able to talk about where it's hot and where it's cold; learners are unlikely to be satisfied with half the story. Using the context of a weather map and a limited number of weather and temperature words (five to eight at a time), learners can use their own mnemonic learning strategies to both connect the images to the words and process the antonyms. In addition to working with thematic stories

The introductory semantic word lists on the *OPD* intro pages help learners focus on high-frequency words.

A thematic presentation of the vocabulary (in this case a day at the park) provides a framework for including semantic and thematic sets in the lesson.

The Body, OPD *pages 104–105*

and limited numbers of related words, we can also be sure to provide practice activities that prompt learners to use new language in a variety of modalities, making it more likely that one of those modalities will help the word "stick."

The thematic approach

In a thematic presentation, the target vocabulary words are linked to the theme of the lesson rather than to each other. Instead of learning a list of colors or clothing items, for example, learners could be presented with a story or picture story on online shopping. Their attention would be drawn to vocabulary such as *dark blue, red, sweater, medium, on sale, website, order number, gift, secure,* and *shipping*. Thematic instruction is well suited to a competency-based curriculum. Adult learners can focus on themes of apartment hunting, problems on the job, parent-teacher conferences, etc. Thematic instruction can also be based on academic content, such as themes in history like colonization or the Industrial Revolution.

Approaching an illustration as a story is probably the simplest way to integrate a thematic vocabulary approach across ESL levels. The story page below (pages 122–123 in the *OPD*) shows an example of vocabulary instruction using both semantic and thematic sets. The illustration

of a health fair depicts a number of words associated with health and nutrition in addition to words that one might use in a variety of settings, such as *booth* and *demonstration*. A simple story shows the key vocabulary in context and integrates words that were presented earlier in the dictionary (e.g., *blood pressure gauge, medical care, cook, free,* etc.) By providing this balance of linked and unlinked words, learners can approximate an authentic reading experience in which at least 90 percent of the vocabulary is known and the remaining ten percent is supported by the word list.

> **TASK:** Find an illustration in a magazine, Web site, or book that is relevant to your learners. Write a short script you could use to present the target vocabulary to the learners.

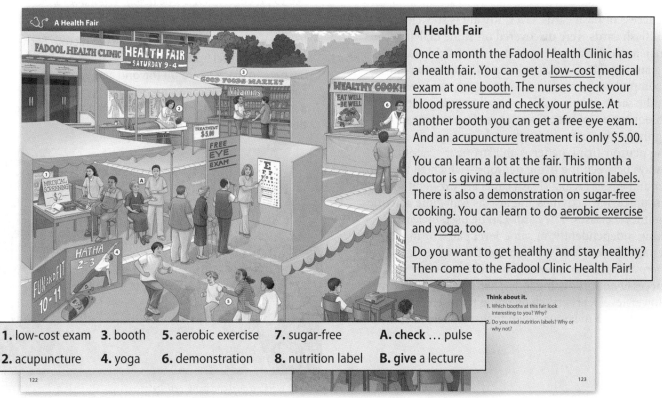

A Health Fair, OPD pages 122–123

The vocabulary continuum

The beauty of language instruction is that every lesson we teach continuously exposes learners to new vocabulary and allows them to work with the words they've learned previously. In the previous section of this book, we worked with ways to explicitly present and practice vocabulary using communicative lessons and picture dictionaries. In this section, we'll look at multilevel vocabulary activities that can be integrated into various stages of the lesson and adapted for learners' needs and proficiency levels. The five basic activity types we'll examine are:

- Picture flash cards
- Word flash cards
- Roundtable brainstorming, labeling, and writing
- Information exchanges
- Focused listening

> **REFLECTION:** What kinds of flash card activities have you tried as a language learner? How have you used flash cards in your classes? What are the advantages and disadvantages of flash cards?

Flash card activities

The success of flash cards as a study aid is so well known that if flash cards were discovered on stone tablets in an ancient ruin somewhere, many in our field would shrug and say, "But of course!" Yet the ability to read and comprehend a new word once is not, as we've seen, the same as being able to recall or recognize it in a subsequent encounter. Creating numerous "recall/recognize" encounters through flash cards produces strong neuron-firing patterns and stronger synaptic pathways between the firing neurons—which all leads to easier and easier recall.[11] Flash cards are excellent for pair warm-up/review activities and also as wait-time activities in multilevel classes. The cards can be used by learners working independently, in same-level pairs, or in mixed-level pairs. Lower-level learners can test higher-level learners and can get exposure to new vocabulary without the necessity of producing it. Higher-level learners can test lower-level learners, challenging themselves to provide clues to meaning when their partners need help.

Picture flash cards

Picture flash cards are excellent for all levels because they create a visual association with the word or phrase being studied. There are several ways to make sets of picture flash cards—for instance, learners can select words they want to study, write them on the back of index cards, then cut matching images from magazines and paste them to front of the cards. Learners can also draw their own images on the index cards, or you can have learners cut apart a set of reproducible picture cards and write the matching words on the back.

Learners can use picture flash cards in any of the following ways:

- Partner A shows the picture card and Partner B identifies the associated word or phrase.
- Partner A picks from a set of noun cards and acts out the word for one or more partners who try to guess it.
- Partner A picks from a set of verb cards and acts out the word. Partner B identifies the action. (For example, Partner A picks up a card that shows the verb *run*, so she runs in place. Partner B says, *You're running*.)
- Have learners work in groups of four with an actor, a director and two audience members. The actor picks the card and acts out the verb. The director asks the audience one of four questions depending on the structure you'd like to practice: *What is s/he doing? What does s/he like to do? What did s/he do? What can s/he do?*
- Partners have identical grids and sets of picture flash cards that they conceal from each other. Partner A tells Partner B where to place a card on the grid and Partner A puts her card in the same location on her grid. Partners have to do a lot of clarification and active listening to have their grids be identical at the end of the activity.

Learners working on a grid game activity.

- Partners sit side by side with their picture cards shuffled on their desks. Partner A's flash cards are laid out picture side up; Partner B's flash cards are word side up. Partner A begins by picking up one of his cards, naming it, and putting it above his set of cards, Partner B picks the matching word card and does the same. The partners check the other sides of their cards to see if they have a match. If they do, the cards stay up at the top. If not, they go back down with the other cards. The partners continue practicing until all the pictures and words are matched.

- Learners in small groups take turns picking a card and giving a definition that doesn't use the word (e.g., *You use this to water the plants.*) Everyone in the group tries to guess the word (*sprinklers? hose?*). Note: This activity is very challenging and is an effective way for higher-level learners to expand on basic vocabulary.

Word flash cards

Word flash cards generally have the target word on one side and the definition, a synonym, an example, a collocation, or another clue on the reverse side. For example, a learner who wants to remember words associated with computers and the Internet might have the following words and cues on his cards:

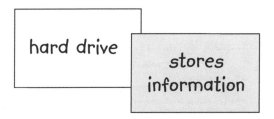

Front of card	Back of card	Focus
hard drive	stores information	definition
tower	CPU	synonym
Web site	weather.com	example
link	*Click on a _____.*	collocation

Another strategy in creating word flash cards is to use different colors to help learners recall definitions and parts of speech: verbs on green cards, nouns on blue cards, adjectives on white cards, adverbs on yellow cards, and so on.

The same activities that learners can do with picture flash cards can be done with word flash cards as well.

Teaching learners to make flash cards is one way to engage them in their own vocabulary development. If possible, help learners hole-punch their flash cards and collect them on a binder ring.

> **TASK:** Prepare for and conduct a picture flash card or word flash card activity in your class.
>
> - Determine which words learners will study.
>
> - Determine how they will prepare the cards.
>
> - Select an activity that will work well with the target vocabulary and your learners' levels.
>
> - Prepare materials that will help you model the activity for the class (e.g., oversize picture cards that can be seen from the back of the class, or picture cards on overhead transparencies).

Roundtable activities

A roundtable activity is a cooperative learning activity in which small groups of learners take turns contributing what they know or think to a single worksheet. This activity type is extremely well suited to vocabulary practice and has social, cognitive, and mnemonic strategies built in.

In a roundtable activity, learners sit around a table or with their desks pulled close together and pass a paper and pen around the group. Having the learners share the single sheet of paper and the pen encourages positive interdependence. Having each person contribute his or her ideas to the paper ensures individual accountability. The roundtable activities detailed below—roundtable brainstorm, roundtable label, and roundtable write—can be used to review, pre-assess, check comprehension, or practice vocabulary that supports the lesson objective.

Roundtable brainstorm

This version of the roundtable can be used with almost no preparation. Learners work in groups of four to generate as many words on a given topic as they can within a time limit. As they pass the paper from one learner to the next, each person says a word and then writes it on the paper. If a learner can't think of a word, he or she can say, "Pass," or ask for an idea from the group. Once time is called, groups report the results of their roundtable brainstorm to create a class vocabulary list. This provides an excellent whole-class overview of what learners already know and helps individual learners quickly identify gaps in their basic vocabulary.

Roundtable label

In the roundtable label activity, learners take turns labeling a set of pictures or a scene on a sheet of paper that's passed around the group. For pre-assessment, comprehension check, and guided practice, the picture should include the words to be targeted in the main lesson. For review, any previously learned vocabulary can be used. While spelling is not the focus during the labeling, learners can certainly ask each other for spelling help as they write, and once all the words the group knows have been labeled, learners should be encouraged to check their spelling in their dictionaries.

You can create your own worksheet with a scene and blank labels or use a ready-made one. An alternative is to ask each group to open a single picture dictionary to a large scene and have them mask the word list. Then have the group members take turns naming an item from the scene and writing its number on the paper that is passed around the group.

Roundtable write

In the roundtable write, learners take turns writing sentences about a scene. The sentences may or may not connect to form a paragraph, depending on the proficiency level of the learners. The scene should be related to the lesson and may be a prompt for target vocabulary or a review of previously learned vocabulary.

Low-intermediate groups can first generate sentences about the picture and then work together to edit the sentences to create a more unified story. Beginners can practice a grammar structure using the target vocabulary, writing as many sentences they can about the scene. Low-literacy learners can use the picture as a language-experience writing prompt, telling their story to a higher-level classmate who writes it for them. At every level, the incorporation of target vocabulary into a meaningful written narrative is an important step in vocabulary development.

Information exchanges

The activities that fall under the umbrella of information exchange are those in which pairs work with different sets of information, asking and answering questions to determine which information they need from each other. These activities are usually structured to practice the

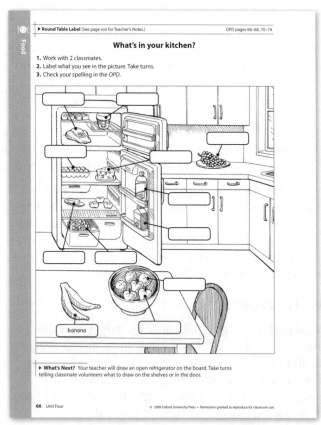

A roundtable label from Classic Classroom Activities *page 66*

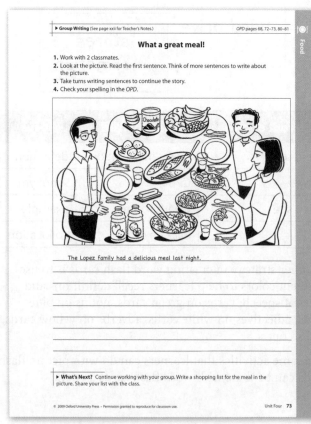

A roundtable write from Classic Classroom Activities *page 73*

vocabulary and grammar from a lesson; however, there is an element of spontaneity in the exchanges, as learners can also make use of other language they've learned to get the information they need. In this way, information exchanges foster both the production and ownership stages of vocabulary development.

Many types of information exchange activities exist, including:

Information gap

Partner A has one-third of the information, Partner B has another one-third, and they share the last third. For example, if both partners had weather maps, Partner A's map might show the weather in six cities, and B's map might have the weather in six cities, but they would only have three cities in common. To complete the activity, learners need to ask and answer questions to fill in the weather conditions that are missing from their maps.

Picture differences

Partner A has a picture and Partner B has the same picture but with a certain number of differences. Learners describe their pictures to each other in order to determine what the differences are.

Drawing dictation

Partner A describes a picture to Partner B so that she can draw it. Once Partner B has drawn the picture according to Partner A's directions, the learners reverse roles and Partner B describes a new picture for Partner A to draw.

Focused listening

In the classroom, learner comprehension often becomes dependent on an instructor's voice and mannerisms. Outside the classroom, the natural speed, intonation and dialects that await learners often interfere with their ability to recognize words and phrases they have already learned. Focused listening activities help bridge that gap for learners by providing exposure to voices speaking at natural speed with an approximation of the natural interruptions and "noise" that occur in real life listening exchanges. In a lesson on the topic of weather, for example, learners could listen to two people talking about plans related to the weather or watch a video clip of a TV weather report. The learners practice listening for known information (the weather conditions) embedded in language they may or may not know.

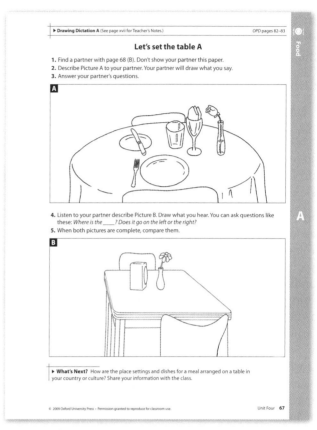

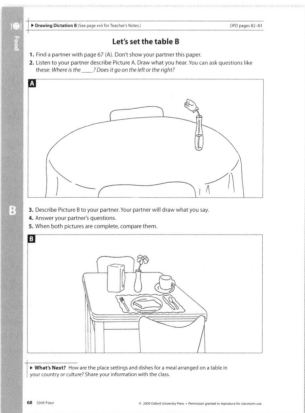

An information gap from Classic Classroom Activities *pages 67–68*

Integrating Vocabulary Activities into Instruction

The skills employed in this type of practice mimic the skills we employ in real-life listening:

- Predicting what we will hear
- Listening with expectations
- Adjusting our expectations
- Clarifying what we hear

There are many pre-recorded CDs developed for this purpose, and the procedure for conducting a focused listening activity is fairly straightforward.

First, review the language learners will be listening for. Next, set the context (to help build expectations, and prompt predictions.) After that, explain the listening task (e.g., listen for the temperature, circle the weather conditions, match the city and the weather). Play an example from the recording so that learners understand the task. Finally, play the listening passage and have learners listen for the target language. Get their feedback on what they heard, and have the class reach consensus on what was said by replaying the passage as needed. If the class hears two different words, write both on the board to "focus the listening." Point out clues such as the number of syllables in each word, the starting and ending sounds, and the associated phrases that one would hear with each word. Then play that section of the passage again, so learners can more clearly hear which word is said.

It's a good idea to follow up a focused listening activity with an information exchange or other learner-to-learner listening and speaking activity so that learners can apply the listening skills they've learned to their own interactions. For example, after learners listen to a weather report for weather conditions, they can engage in an information exchange using pairs of weather maps, each presenting different weather information.

Focused listening exercises are excellent for multilevel instruction. The same listening script can be used for all levels, but learners at different levels can be given different tasks. The tasks should always be simple, however, because the act of listening in a second language is very demanding. Low beginners can sequence, check, or circle the information they hear. High beginners can do the same or do completion or matching tasks with the support of a word box. And low-intermediate learners can take notes on the key information that they hear.

TASK: Use the listening passage below (from the *OPD* weather unit) or select another listening passage and identify which words learners will be listening for and which words could be difficult for them to hear. Think of a task that learners could do to document their listening (e.g., circle, underline, or check an item on a worksheet, take notes, or draw a picture).

1. Now for the national forecast. Take a look at Southern California. It's sunny and clear with temperatures around 90 degrees. Can you believe it? They're having a heat wave in March!

2. Farther east, in Utah and Colorado, the temperatures are in the 50s. It's cool and cloudy, but it's not raining today.

3. In Illinois, it's still raining and it's cold. It's also foggy in many locations. You could see a thunderstorm later this afternoon.

4. And in New York it's snowing again. The snowstorm should end this afternoon, but the temperatures will be cold. Be careful on those icy streets tomorrow.

REFLECTION: Where do your learners hear English spoken? How could you incorporate that kind of listening in your instruction?

Vocabulary Development through Reading

The vocabulary-reading connection

Although the link between vocabulary and reading has been mentioned numerous times in this book, it merits greater development. Native speakers owe the majority of their vocabulary to their extensive reading. Considering that approximately 90 percent of our conversations use a mere 2,000 words,[12] it's not surprising that we would turn to written material for a richer source of vocabulary development.

Using reading as a tool to increase vocabulary is important across all levels. Intermediate and advanced ESL learners who have a basic vocabulary of approximately 3,000 words are in a good position to start expanding their vocabulary through reading. But reading is important for beginners' vocabulary development as well. The difference for these lower-level learners is that they need texts adapted for their language level, with a limited number of new words presented within the context of words that are known.

When looking for reading materials to build learners' literacy and vocabulary skills, remember that the reading passages need to match learners' needs and interests as well as their comprehension level. You'll also want to look for materials that include comprehension checks and pre-reading and post-reading activities, and that recycle vocabulary from one passage to the next. When possible, use a reading lesson as the last in a series of lessons on a topic or competency. This gives learners the chance to reencounter words they've learned and to use some of those words to understand the new words in the text. For multilevel classes, consider taking a high-beginning-level reading and adapting it up for intermediates and down for low beginners, so that all three groups are reading about the same general topic.[13]

Pre-reading vocabulary activities

Pre-reading activities prepare readers for the text by activating their prior knowledge, helping them identify their purpose in reading, and preparing them with the key vocabulary and concepts they'll need to understand the material. A roundtable brainstorm (see page 27) is a good tool for identifying learners' prior knowledge and identifying words they need to learn. Another option is to put key words from the reading passage on the board and ask learners to collaboratively identify those words they know and those they don't. Elicit the meanings for the known words and teach the unknown ones. Put clues to meaning on the board beside the words and encourage learners to refer to the list as they read.

Reading and the unknown word

When learners read a passage, they almost always come across words that they either don't recognize or never knew. To keep the reading experience as authentic as possible, and to allow the learners to build reading fluency, encourage them to read through the passage once for the gist of the author's ideas. Rather than telling learners to skip over words they don't know, ask them to highlight, *but not look up*, the words they don't understand.

Once learners have read through the text silently, ask a few key comprehension questions about the passage and then elicit any unfamiliar words the class encountered. Carefully pronounce and write these words near the "new vocabulary" list. Encourage learners to help each other with the meanings of unknown words. Where words are related to words already taught, show the connection. This is also a good time for the class to look up words in a dictionary and work with multiple definitions.

Once the distracting unknown words are understood, have learners read the passage a second time, again silently. You can read the passage aloud for a third exposure to the text, with learners following along.

Post-reading vocabulary activities

Pre-reading and reading will strengthen learners' comprehension of new vocabulary, but without further practice it is unlikely that they will be able to recall, recognize, or produce the new words. Some post-reading activities that build retention and give learners an opportunity to produce the words as they talk and write about the text are as follows:

- Using target vocabulary to summarize the passage
- Writing the new words in a vocabulary notebook and using a sentence from the passage as an example
- Completing sentences using a target word family
- Using the new words to write a short response to the reading

> **TASK:** Select a reading that is at your learners' level and identify the key words that you will want to teach during pre-reading. Develop a pre-reading and a post-reading exercise to help teach and practice the new vocabulary.

The magic of point-and-click

Vocabulary learning software has many applications in our field, but among its finest attributes are its infinite patience and its ability to repeat the same word or phrase with identical inflection every time. With the limitations of classroom instruction time and the difficult and exhausting lives led by so many of our learners, it's hard for beginning learners to get the practice needed to develop a large active vocabulary. Effective vocabulary software can work with different vocabulary learning strategies and take learners through the five stages of vocabulary development. The immediate feedback that learners receive from these programs allows them to gauge their progress, which in turn motivates them to continue practicing.

When a learner first explores new vocabulary in an interactive program, text is linked to visual and audio input. This link helps promote mnemonic association and comprehension. The addition of video scenes to a computer program makes the presentation of new language even more dynamic. Most programs also offer a variety of cognitive practice activities to build retention, such as listening and matching, dictation, and drag-and-drop sentence completion. Interactive cloze activities such as the one shown below provide kinesthetic learning and help build learners' retention and recognition of target vocabulary.

OPD Interactive *software*

Programs that include listening and reading activities give learners the opportunity to recognize vocabulary out of the original context. In order for learners to get sufficient practice in producing the new language, software should also include speaking and writing activities. These activities might include conversation practice activities in which users record and compare their speech to an accurate model, or writing prompts based on the target vocabulary or topic. When writing activities include hyperlinks to a dictionary or online search engines, learners can make use of determination strategies in order to express themselves.

Intrapersonal and interpersonal learning

Perhaps the biggest difference between computer-based and classroom-based instruction is the way vocabulary software allows learners to use their metacognitive strategies. Putting the learner in charge of how and when vocabulary is learned creates individualized practice. Interactive exercises and quizzes, also part of most software packages, allow learners to engage in self-testing, another metacognitive strategy.

Although classroom instruction does offer far more opportunities for authentic interaction and meaningful communication tasks, interactive software can provide the social aspect of vocabulary learning when users play vocabulary learning games in pairs or small groups. Vocabulary games are extremely motivating across levels and age groups. While presentation software for LCD projectors and SmartBoards is still in limited use in adult ESL programs, its appeal is growing. This powerful teaching tool combines the best aspects of both software and classroom instruction. Using these tools, the entire class can take part in interactive vocabulary exercises and games.

> **REFLECTION:** If you had presentation software and could conduct any of the activities discussed in this *Handbook* with your whole class, which ones would you choose? Why?

Where do I go from here?

By this point you've thought a lot about vocabulary development and how it pertains to your learners' needs. You've reflected on the ideas and activities presented here and possibly refined some of your instructional techniques and strategies.

Of course, there is always more to learn, and new vocabulary research is being carried out even as you read. The vocabulary notebook suggestions below, as well as the lesson planning templates on the following pages, will support you as you continue to explore ways to help your learners understand, remember, and own more and more English!

Vocabulary notebooks

To help learners expand their vocabulary development beyond the walls of the classroom, encourage them to make flash cards and to keep vocabulary notebooks. (See page 26 for ideas on ways to make flash cards and incorporate them into your lessons.)

Vocabulary notebooks encourage the practice of all five types of vocabulary learning strategies. Determination strategies are used when the learner looks up the definition of the word and identifies its part of speech or analyzes it in the notebook entry. Mnemonic strategies can come into play if the learner puts an image or a word association in the notebook, and cognitive strategies are used in organizing the information in separate notebook sections. Learners use metacognitive strategies as they determine which words to record and use the notebook as a self-study tool. As the notebook can also be worked on or studied with a partner, it encourages social strategies as well.

One style of vocabulary notebook, featured in Keith Folse's *Vocabulary Myths*, has four elements per entry: the word itself, its translation, its definition, and an example of the word in a phrase or a collocation.

remember (word)	recuerde (translation)
to bring to, mind, recall (definition)	Remember to study new words! (example)

While flash cards make it possible to practice recalling the target word with one of these elements, a vocabulary notebook set up in this way encourages learners to practice recalling the target vocabulary with four different prompts. To do so, learners can create a mask that is two cells high on one side, and only one cell high on the other. They have only to turn or flip the mask and a different prompt is revealed to help the recall the word and its meaning.

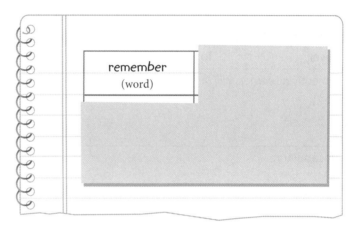

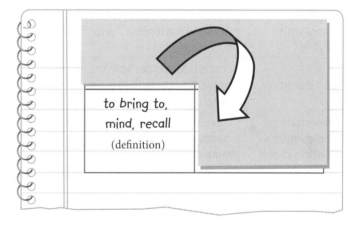

Creating notebook assignments

After learners have started creating their notebooks outside of class and are comfortable entering information about a word, you can encourage them to use the notebooks to learn words they hear in their daily lives. Elicit a list of situations where learners can look for or listen for new words (e.g., documents, billboards, search engines, food packaging, television shows). Next, ask learners to write a simple statement on the inside cover of their notebooks that states how many words per week they commit to recording and defining in the notebook. This simple goal-setting task can have a tremendous effect on the motivation of learners to continue their vocabulary development on their own.

Additional Resources

Single-level lesson planner

The template below is for a single-level class. You may want to start your planning by identifying the lesson objective and determining which grammar structures and vocabulary items support that objective. Next, you'll need a communication task and evaluation activity that demonstrates achievement of the objective. Plan the warm-up/review, presentation, and practice stages by identifying what learners need to listen for, say, read, and write in order to successfully complete the communication task or evaluation. Finally, determine what application and closing activities are needed. Remember that it is essential to match the objective, presentation, and evaluation and to include activities that develop both accuracy and fluency skill development activities in every lesson.

Single-level lesson planning template		
Level:	Topic:	*OPD* page(s)
Objective: *Learners will be able to*		
Vocabulary:		Grammar:

Stage	Goals	Activities / Resources
Warm-up / Review	Activate the learners' prior knowledge.	
Introduction	Focus learners on how the lesson objective meets their language needs.	
Presentation and comprehension check	Develop and then check learner's comprehension of target language and concepts.	
Guided practice	Build retention of the new language and provide opportunities to develop accuracy in producing the new language.	
Communicative practice*	Provide opportunities to focus on fluent production of the new language by completing an authentic communication task.	
Evaluation*	Assess learners' accuracy and fluency in producing and responding to the new language.	
Application*	Provide a class or homework activity to help learners recognize and work with the new language in a new context or proficiency area.	
Closing	Help learners process their progress toward their goals.	

*Note: Any two or three of these stages can be collapsed for performance-based assessment.

Multilevel lesson planner

In the multilevel planning template below, the goals for each stage of a multilevel lesson are included. (See page 10 for the general goals of each lesson stage.) Beginning and ending each class with a whole class activity underscores the importance of class community in an environment where there are disparate proficiency levels and varied needs. And while mixed-level activities make the most of the learners' varied interests and abilities, it is also important to provide same-level activities so that learners at all levels can have their individual language needs met. (See page 16 for multilevel resources.)

Multilevel lesson planning template		
Levels:	Topic:	*OPD* page(s):
Objectives Level A: Level B: Level C:		
Vocabulary: Level A: Level B: Level C:	Grammar: Level A: Level B: Level C:	

Stage	Goals	Activities / Resources		
Warm-up / Review	Build class community. Focus the class on the topic. (whole class)			
Introduction, presentation, and comprehension check	Provide visual and contextual support to ensure all learners' comprehension of the general lesson. Use leveled questions to check comprehension of the target language and concepts for each level. (whole class with mini-presentations as needed)			
Guided practice	Provide opportunities for each level to accurately produce the language that supports their level objectives. (same-level groups)	Level A	Level B	Level C
Communicative practice*	Provide opportunities to focus on fluent production of the new language by completing an authentic communication task. (mixed-level groups)	Mixed levels: _____		Same level: _____
Evaluation*	Assess learners' accuracy and fluency in achieving their level-specific objectives. (same-level groups)	Level A	Level B	Level C
Application*	Provide application or expansion activities that relate to their level's objectives. (mixed- or same-level groups)	Mixed levels: _____ or Same level: _____		
Closing	Re-establish class community. (whole class)			

* Note: Any two or three of these stages can be collapsed for performance-based assessment.

Pre-assessment and goal-setting worksheets

Research in learner persistence shows that needs-based instruction and goal setting dramatically affects learners' success.[14] The two worksheets below will help your students first identify the words they need to learn and then commit to learning them. (See page 11 for ideas on how to use these materials.)

Vocabulary pre-assessment survey

- Copy the list of target words into the first column.
- Check the column that is true for you for each word.

Target Word	This is the first time I've seen this word.	I understand and use this word.	I need this word in my vocabulary.	I don't need this word right now.

Vocabulary goal setting sheet

VOCABULARY GOAL FOR THE WEEK OF _____ / _____ / _____ **TO** _____ / _____ / _____

My target words this week:

1. _____
2. _____
3. _____
4. _____
5. _____

6. _____
7. _____
8. _____
9. _____
10. _____

I will use the following studying techniques. Circle all that apply:

- flash cards
- labeling
- computer practice

- listening practice (MP3 player, CD)
- workbook exercises
- other _____

Goal Assessment: Number of words learned = _____   Initial _____

Endnotes

1. NCSALL, *How Teachers Change: A Study of Professional Development in Adult Education.*
   http://www.ncsall.net/research/report25.pdf

2. Paul Nation and Robert Waring, "Vocabulary Size, Text Coverage, and Word Lists," in *Vocabulary: Description, Acquisition, and Pedagogy*, ed. Norbert Schmitt and Michael McCarthy (Cambridge: Cambridge University Press, 1997), 6–19. This article is also available at http://www1.harenet.ne.jp/~waring/papers/cup.html.

3. *Merriam-Webster's Collegiate Dictionary*, 11th ed. (Springfield, Massachusetts: Merriam-Webster, Incorporated, 2003).

4. Laurie Bauer and Paul Nation, "Word Families," *International Journal of Lexicography* 6, no. 4 (1993): 253–279.

5. Andreea Cervatiuc, "ESL Vocabulary Acquisition: Target and Approach," *ITESLJ* 14, no. 1 (January 2008). http://iteslj.org/Articles/Cervatiuc-VocabularyAcquisition.html

6. Ibid.

7. See "Useful Web sites" on page 39 of this *Handbook* for links to word lists mentioned in this section.

8. Batia Laufer, "Learning Vocabulary in a Second Language: What do we know about it from Research?" (paper presented at the national conference of the Centre for Multicultural Education [NAFO], Tromso, Norway, June 2006). http://www.hio.no/content/view/full/45377

9. Norbert Schmitt and Michael McCarthy, eds., *Vocabulary: Description, Acquisition, and Pedagogy* (Cambridge: Cambridge University Press, 1997).

10. Robert Waring, "The Negative Effects of Learning Words in Semantic Sets," *System* 25, no. 2 (1997): 261–274; Thomas Tinkham, "The Effect of Semantic and Thematic Clustering on the Learning of Second Language Vocabulary," *Second Language Research* 13, no. 2 (1997): 138–163.

11. "Want to Improve Memory? Strengthen Your Synapses. Here's How," *Medical News Today*, 11 January 2007. http://www.medicalnewstoday.com/articles/60455.php

12. Schonell, F. J., et al., *A Study of the Oral Vocabulary of Adults* (Brisbane: University of Queensland Press, 1956).

13. See "Readers linked to picture dictionaries" on page 39 of this *Handbook* for a list of suggested readers.

14. John Comings, Andrea Parella, and Lisa Soricone, "Helping Adults Persist: Four Supports," *Focus on Basics*, 4, issue A (March 2000).

References

Works cited

Bauer, Laurie, and Paul Nation. "Word Families." *International Journal of Lexicography* 6, no. 4 (1993): 253–279.

Cervatiuc, Andreea. "ESL Vocabulary Acquisition: Target and Approach," *ITESLJ* 14, no. 1 (January 2008). http://iteslj.org/Articles/Cervatiuc-VocabularyAcquisition.html.

Comings, John, Andrea Parrella, and Lisa Soricone. (2000, March). "Helping Adults Persist: Four Supports." *Focus on Basics* 4, issue A (March 2000). http://www.ncsall.net/?id=332

Folse, Keith S. *Vocabulary Myths: Applying Second Language Research to Classroom Teaching.* Ann Arbor: University of Michigan Press, 2004.

Gairns, Ruth, and Stuart Redman. *Working with Words: A Guide to Teaching and Learning Vocabulary.* Cambridge: Cambridge University Press, 1986.

Laufer, Batia. "Learning Vocabulary in a Second Language: What do we know about it from Research?" Paper presented at the national conference of the Centre for Multicultural Education (NAFO), Tromso, Norway, June 2006. http://www.hio.no/content/view/full/45377

Merriam-Webster's Collegiate Dictionary. 11th ed. Springfield, Massachusetts: Merriam-Webster, Incorporated, 2003.

Nation, I. S. P. *Learning Vocabulary in Another Language.* Cambridge: Cambridge University Press, 2001.

Nation, Paul, and Robert Waring. "Vocabulary Size, Text Coverage, and Word Lists." In *Vocabulary: Description, Acquisition, and Pedagogy*, edited by Norbert Schmitt and Michael McCarthy, 6–19. Cambridge: Cambridge University Press, 1997.

NCSALL. *How Teachers Change: A Study of Professional Development in Adult Education.* http://ncsall.net/research/report25.pdf

Parrish, Betsy. *Teaching Adult ESL: A Practical Introduction.* New York: McGraw-Hill, 2004.

Savage, K. Lynn, ed. *Teacher Training Through Video: ESL Techniques—Early Production.* White Plains: Longman Publishing Group, 1993.

Schmitt, Norbert. *Vocabulary in Language Teaching.* Cambridge: Cambridge University Press, 2000.

Schonell, F. J., et al. *A study of the Oral Vocabulary of Adults.* Brisbane: University of Queensland Press, 1956.

Tinkham, Thomas. "The Effect of Semantic and Thematic Clustering on the Learning of Second Language Vocabulary." *Second Language Research* 13, no. 2 (1997): 138–163.

"Want to Improve Memory? Strengthen Your Synapses. Here's How." *Medical News Today.* 11 January 2007. http://www.medicalnewstoday.com/articles/60455.php

Waring, Robert. "The Negative Effects of Learning Words in Semantic Sets." *System* 25, no. 2 (1997): 261–274.

Further reading on vocabulary development

Coady, James. "Research on ESL/EFL Vocabulary Acquisition: Putting It in Context." In *Second Language Reading and Vocabulary Learning*, edited by Thomas Huckin, Margot Haynes, and James Coady, 3–23. Norwood, NJ: Ablex, 1993.

DeCarrico, Jeanette S. "Vocabulary Learning and Teaching." In *Teaching English as a Second or Foreign Language*, 3rd ed., edited by Marianne Celce-Murcia, 285–299. Boston: Heinle & Heinle, 2001.

de la Fuente, María José. "Negotiation and Oral Acquisition of L2 Vocabulary: The Roles of Input and Output in the Receptive and Productive Acquisition of Words." *Studies in Second Language Acquisition* 24 (2002): 81–112

Ellis, Rod. *The Study Of Second Language Acquisition.* Oxford: Oxford University Press. 1994.

Gass, Susan M., and María José.Alvarez Torres. "Attention When? An Investigation of the Ordering Effect of Input and Interaction." *Studies in Second Language Acquisition* 27 (2005): 1–31.

Henriksen, Brigit. "Three Dimensions Of Vocabulary Development." *Studies in Second Language Acquisition* 21, no. 2 (1999): 303–317.

Nation, I. S. P. "Vocabulary." In *Practical English Language Teaching*, edited by David Nunan, 129–152. New York: McGraw-Hill, 2003.

Prince, Peter. "Second Language Vocabulary Learning: The Role of Context Versus Translations as a Function of Proficiency." *Modern Language Journal* 80, no. 4 (1996): 478–493.

Smith, Carl B. *Vocabulary Instruction and Reading Comprehension.* Bloomington, Ind.: ERIC Clearinghouse on Reading, English, and Communication, 1997, ERIC, ED 412506.

Further reading on the role of vocabulary in reading skill development

Burt, Miriam, Joy Kreeft Peyton and Rebecca Adams. *Reading and Adult English Language Learners: A Review of the Research.* Washington, D.C.: Center for Applied Linguistics, 2003.

Grabe, William. "Foundations for Reading Assessment." Paper presented at the 2nd Language Testing and Evaluation Forum, Athens, Greece, June 2006. http://testingforum.hau.gr/docs/W.Grabehandout-OK.pdf.

Koda, Keiko. *Insights into Second Language Reading: A Cross-Linguistic Approach.* Cambridge: Cambridge University Press, 2005.

National Center for ESL Literacy Education Staff. *Adult English Language Instruction in the 21st Century.* Washington, D.C.: Center for Applied Linguistics, 2003.

National Reading Panel. *Teaching Children to Read: An Evidence-Based Assessment of the Scientific Research Literature on Reading and Its Implications on Reading Instruction*, 2000. http://www.nationalreadingpanel.org/Publications/summary.htm

Further reading on the role of visuals in language lessons

Illinois Resource Center. *ESL and Bilingual Teachers Toolkit: Methods and Strategies—Instructional Methods for All Students.* Arlington Heights, Illinois: Illinois Resource Center, 2005. http://www.thecenterlibrary.org/cwis/cwisdocs/methods-all.html

van der Werff, Joep. "Using Pictures from Magazines." *ITESLJ* 9, no. 7 (July 2003). http://iteslj.org/Techniques/Werff-Pictures.html

Wood, Karen D., and Josefina Tinajero. "Using Pictures to Teach Content to Second Language Learners." *Middle School Journal* 33, no. 5 (2002): 47–51. http://www.nmsa.org/Publications/MiddleSchoolJournal/May2002/Article7/tabid/423/Default.aspx

Adult ESL picture dictionaries and lesson plans

Oxford Picture Dictionary Program

Adelson-Goldstein, Jayme, and Norma Shapiro. *The Oxford Picture Dictionary.* 2nd ed. New York: Oxford University Press, 2008.

Santamaria, Jenni Currie, et al. *The Oxford Picture Dictionary Lesson Plans.* 2nd ed. New York: Oxford University Press, 2008.

Basic Oxford Picture Dictionary

Gramer, Margot F. *The Basic Oxford Picture Dictionary.* 2nd ed. New York: Oxford University Press, 2003.

Brod, Shirley, and Garnet Templin-Imel. *The Basic Oxford Picture Dictionary Literacy Program.* 2nd ed. New York: Oxford University Press, 1996.

Adelson-Goldstein, Jayme and Norma Shapiro. *The Basic Oxford Picture Dictionary Teacher's Book.* New York: Oxford University Press, 2003.

Readers linked to picture dictionaries

Howard, Lori. *Read All About It: Levels 1 and 2.* New York: Oxford University Press, 2000.

Ianuzzi, Susan, and Renee Weiss. *Read All About It: Starter.* New York: Oxford University Press, 2005.

The OPD Reading Library. New York: Oxford University Press, 2008.

Multilevel materials for interactive and communicative vocabulary practice

Armstrong, Fiona, et al. *The Basic Oxford Picture Dictionary: Teacher's Resource Book.* 2nd ed. New York: Oxford University Press, 1994.

Mahdesian, Chris. *Step Forward Multilevel Activity Book: Introductory Level.* New York: Oxford University Press, 2008.

———. *Step Forward Multilevel Activity Book: Level 1.* New York: Oxford University Press, 2006.

———. *Step Forward Multilevel Activity Book: Level 4.* New York: Oxford University Press, 2007.

O'Sullivan, Jill Korey. *Step Forward Multilevel Activity Book: Level 3.* New York: Oxford University Press, 2007.

Santopietro Weddel, Kathleen. *Step Forward Introductory Level Literacy Reproducible Book.* New York: Oxford University Press, 2008.

Wagner, Sandy. *Step Forward Multilevel Activity Book: Level 2.* New York: Oxford University Press, 2006.

Weiss, Renee, et al. *The Oxford Picture Dictionary: Classic Classroom Activities.* 2nd ed. New York: Oxford University Press, 2008.

Useful Web sites

The Academic Word List. http://language.massey.ac.nz/staff/awl/headwords.shtml

Center for Adult English Language Acquisition (CAELA). http://www.cal.org/caela/

Center for Applied Linguistics (CAL). http://www.cal.org/

The Dolch Basic Word List. http://www.english-zone.com/reading/dolch.html

The Fry Reading Vocabulary List. http://www.usu.edu/teachall/text/reading/Frylist.pdf

The General Service Word List (revision). http://jbauman.com/gsl.html

The Internet TESL Journal. http://iteslj.org/

The University Word List. http://jbauman.com/aboutUWL.html